Fastest Machines

Inquiries should be addressed to Raintree Publishers Inc., 205 West Highland Avenue, Milwaukee, Wisconsin 53203.

Library of Congress Number: 80-10227

1 2 3 4 5 6 7 8 9 0 84 83 82 81 80

Printed in the United States of America.

Library of Congress Cataloging in Publication Data

Stevens, Chris.
Fastest machines.

Includes index.
SUMMARY: Describes the machines built and used to break speed records on land, on water, and in the air.
1. Automobiles, Racing—Juvenile literature. 2. Airplanes, Racing—Juvenile literature. 3. Motorboats—Juvenile literature. 4. Speed records—Juvenile literature. [1. Automobiles, Racing. 2. Airplanes, Racing. 3. Motorboats. 4. Speed records] I. Title.
TL236.S74 629.04'6 80-10227

ISBN 0-8172-1337-6 lib. bdg.

Photographs appear through the courtesy of the following:
Aerospatiale (France): pp. 24-25
Airportraits: p. 26
Atlas Van Lines, Inc.: pp. 18-19
Bell Labs: p. 22
Bob Tronolone: pp. 10-11
Consulate General of Japan: pp. 16-17
Department of the Air Force: pp. 26-27
Don Vesco: pp. 13, 14
Firestone: p. 12
Garrett Corp.: p. 15
Goodyear: p. 8
Hurst Performance, Inc.: p. 9
Long Photography: Cover, pp. 4-5
Mobil Oil: p. 21
Pete Farnsworth: pp. 3, 6-7
Rockwell International: pp. 28-29
Sikorsky Aircraft: p. 23
U.S. Equipment Co.: p. 20

fastest MACHINES

Chris Stevens

RAINTREE CHILDRENS BOOKS
Milwaukee • Toronto • Melbourne • London

Fast cars. Fast airplanes. Fast boats. People are fascinated by fast machines. This book has some of the fastest machines in the world.

The machine on this page is the fastest land vehicle. It has a rocket engine. It is the Budweiser Rocket. On December 17, 1979, it went

739.6 miles per hour (1,190.3 kilometers per hour). That is faster than the speed of sound. The Rocket has a computer and other electronic equipment. The Rocket has three solid aluminum wheels. Rubber tires would have broken apart traveling so fast.

For nine years this car was the fastest land vehicle in the world. It is the Blue Flame. Its speed record was 631.4 miles per hour (1,016.1 kilometers per hour). It ran on liquid natural gas. It was also powered by a rocket engine. The only land vehicle faster than the Blue Flame is the Budweiser Rocket.

Norman Craig Breedlove drove the fastest jet-engined car ever built. The car was the Spirit of America—Sonic I. It is over 34 feet (10.4 meters) long. His highest speed in this car was 613.9 miles per hour (987.9 kilometers per hour). He did this on the Bonneville Salt Flats in Utah on November 16, 1965.

The fastest piston-engined car is the Goldenrod. Piston engines are the kind used in regular cars. The Goldenrod had four engines. Its fastest speed was 418.5 miles per hour (673.5 kilometers per hour). Bob Summers drove this car to break what was then the land speed record on November 12, 1965.

The Porsche 917/30 Can Am is the world's fastest racing car. It has reached a speed of 257 miles per hour (413.6 kilometers per hour) on a racetrack in France in 1973.

This car takes only 2.2 seconds to go from 0 to 60 miles per hour (96.6 kilometers per hour). And 12.6 seconds is all the 917/30 takes to get up to 200 miles per hour (321.9 kilometers per hour).

GOODYEAR
SUNOCO
6
SUNOCO
PORSCHE
+AUDI

DieHard
PORSCHE
6
+AUDI
SUNOCO

This jet car is called the Green Monster. In 1964, it was the first jet-engined car to set the land speed record. The Green Monster might have been able to break the record of the Spirit of America. But in 1966, the Green Monster crashed and was destroyed—even though the driver was not hurt.

Here is the Silver Bird. It is the fastest motorcycle of its kind in the world. The Silver Bird is a motorcycle because it has two wheels and a motor. It is 21 feet (6.4 meters) long.

In 1975, the Silver Bird went 303.8 miles per hour (488.9 kilometers per hour). That means it covered a mile in 12 seconds.

This is another fast motorcycle —the Lightning Bolt. In 1978, Marcia Holley drove it 229.4 miles per hour (369.1 kilometers per hour). She set the women's motorcycle speed record.

This is the fastest railroad engine in the world. It is called the LIMRV. The LIMRV is not a passenger train. It was built for the U.S. Department of Transportation as a test vehicle to help improve all trains. In 1974, the LIMRV reached 255 miles per hour (410 kilometers per hour).

This is the world's fastest passenger train. It is part of the Japanese National Railways. This super-express train is called the Shinkansen, which means "new main line." The Shinkansen travels between Tokyo and Osaka. Its average speed is 101.1 miles per hour (162.7 kilometers per hour).

This Gold Cup boat is named the Atlas Van Lines. The Gold Cup is a famous powerboat race that has been held since 1903. In 1978, the Atlas Van Lines went around the Gold Cup course at a speed of 128.3 miles per hour (206.5 kilometers per hour). The boat won the Gold Cup seven times.

Atlas Van Lines

Atlas Van Lines

The Miss U.S. is a powerboat that has several models. The one below is a Gold Cup winner. Another Miss U.S. holds the world speed record for a propeller-driven boat. It is run by an airplane engine, and it went 200 miles per hour (321.9 kilometers per hour).

The Bluebird, on the righthand page, was the first jet speedboat to reach 200 miles per hour. In 1955, it held the then world water speed record of 216.2 miles per hour (347.9 kilometers per hour).

The world speed record for a helicopter was set by this Bell 533. It reached the speed of 316.1 miles per hour (508.7 kilometers per hour). The record is not official, however. That is because the 533 was helped by two turbojet engines.

The official speed record for a regular helicopter was set by this Sikorsky Blackhawk. A regular helicopter has only a rotor engine. The Blackhawk flew 220.9 miles per hour (355.5 kilometers per hour).

The Concorde is the fastest passenger airplane. It flies at a height of about 10 miles (16 kilometers). And its speed is around 1,400 miles per hour (2,250 kilometers per hour).

The plane on the left is Russia's TU-144. It could become the fastest passenger airliner. It is able to fly 1,585 miles per hour (2,550.8 kilometers per hour). So far the TU-144 has reached a speed of about 1,245 miles per hour (2,000 kilometers per hour).

The plane on the right is the Lockheed SR-71. It is the fastest airplane of any kind. It has flown 2,193.2 miles per hour (3,529.6 kilometers per hour). It can reach an altitude of almost 20 miles (32 kilometers).

U.S. AIR FORCE
17958
958

When the Space Shuttle has regular flights in the 1980s, it will become the world's fastest aircraft. The Space Shuttle is part of the United States' space program. It has a crew of three, and it can carry four other people.

The Space Shuttle was first tested on top of a Boeing 747. On regular flights it takes off like a rocket, but it lands like an airplane. The Space Shuttle can fly up to 17,600 miles per hour (28,324 kilometers per hour).

GLOSSARY

engine	A machine that uses energy to run other machines.
helicopter	An aircraft that is kept in the air by blades that rotate above the craft.
jet	A stream of liquid, gas, or vapor that is sent with force through a small opening.
jet car	A car driven by a jet engine.
jet engine	A motor that squirts a liquid or gas in one direction to move a vehicle in the opposite direction.
liquid natural gas	A type of fuel for some rocket engines.
motorcycle	A vehicle with two wheels and an engine.
piston engine	A machine that moves a vehicle by mechanical power. A piston-engine vehicle cannot go as fast as one that has an engine powered by a rocket or a jet.
powerboat	A boat with an engine.
propeller	Blades attached to a hub. When the blades spin in water or air they drive a boat or aircraft forward.
rocket engine	A motor with a device that is driven forward by a stream of hot gases that are let go from the rear.
rotor engine	A motor which drives the blades of a helicopter.
Space Shuttle	A space craft that takes off like a jet and lands like an airplane. It is used to carry scientists and equipment into space.
speedboat	Another name for a powerboat.
turbojet engine	A motor run by a stream of gas or liquid that moves against its blades and turns them.
vehicle	A machine that can carry something.

INDEX